A Human Being Made This

A HUMAN BEING CREATED THIS COMIC

Kathleen Connors

CREATED BY Humans

Published in 2026 by The Rosen Publishing Group, Inc.
2544 Clinton Street, Buffalo, NY 14224

First Edition

Editor: Kristen Nelson
Designer: Michael Flynn

Photo Credits: Cover Tutatamafilm/Shutterstock.com; (series background) Yuliya Chsherbakova/Shutterstock.com; p. 5 nikkimeel/Shutterstock.com; p. 7 Ground Picture/Shutterstock.com; p. 9 Prostock-studio/Shutterstock.com; p. 11 (top) Walter Cicchetti/Shutterstock.com; p. 11 (bottom) https://en.wikipedia.org/wiki/File:Archie_1942_issue_1.jpg; p. 13 GagliardiPhotography/Shutterstock.com; p. 15 (top) catwalker/Shutterstock.com; p. 15 (bottom) Ellianne/Shutterstock.com; p. 17 yayasya/Shutterstock.com; p. 19 VisualArtStudio/Shutterstock.com; p. 21 (girl drawing) StockImageFactory.com/Shutterstock.com; p. 21 (comic border) anak tinta/Shutterstock.com.

Cataloging-in-Publication Data

Names: Connors, Kathleen.
Title: A human being created this comic / Kathleen Connors.
Description: Buffalo, NY : Created by Humans, an imprint of Rosen Publishing, 2026. | Series: A human being made this | Includes glossary and index.
Identifiers: ISBN 9781534552548 (pbk.) | ISBN 9781534552555 (library bound) | ISBN 9781534552562 (ebook)
Subjects: LCSH: Comic books, strips, etc.--Authorship--Juvenile literature. | Comic books, strips, etc.--Juvenile literature. | Comic strip characters--Juvenile literature. | AI art--Juvenile literature.
Classification: LCC PN6710.C659 2026 | DDC 741.51--dc2

Manufactured in China

CPSIA Compliance Information: Batch #QWCBH26. For Further Information contact Rosen Publishing at 1-800-237-9932.

CONTENTS

KID COMIC CREATOR

Do you love to draw and tell stories? Are superheroes or silly animals your favorite things to read about? You might want to create your own comic! A comic is a picture or series of pictures that, when read together, tell a story or joke. It can be one panel or many.

Creating a comic strip or comic book can take its creators days, months, or even years! This kind of work can seem really hard, even if you love comics. Would AI be able to make the process faster or easier?

GET THE FACTS

A panel is one frame or part of a comic strip.

A comic book is many pages of comic strips put together to tell a short story.

GenAI BASICS

AI, or artificial intelligence, is **technology** that can learn. These computer programs "think" like humans. They can find answers to a problem. They can look over lots of data and find patterns in it.

Could AI create a comic? One kind of AI is generative AI, or GenAI. This technology is given lots of data, including pieces of writing and images, or pictures. It uses this data to create something—such as a comic—when given a prompt.

GET THE FACTS

A prompt is the written directions to do something.

A GenAI creation is also only as good as its prompt—which is written by a human!

TO USE OR NOT TO USE?

GenAI is exciting. However, using it to create art has its problems. First, GenAI may use parts of copyrighted works to make the comic. Also, GenAI art sometimes doesn't look quite right. It may not be able to make the same character over and over like a comic would need it to.

The main trouble is this: GenAI comics don't come from the point of view of a cool kid like you! Your ideas and style of drawing are **unique** to you. They are what make a great comic.

GET THE FACTS

Copyrighted content is writing, art, or other creative works that are owned by a person or company. It's illegal to use copyrighted works without permission.

You might enjoy creating comics because they help you **express** how you think or feel about something, like school or sports.

HISTORY OF COMICS

Strips of pictures that tell a story or have a message have been created by humans for hundreds of years. Around the year 1900 in the United States, many of these were meant to be funny. They were called "comic" strips. "Comic" means funny.

Comic books grew up alongside comic strips around the early 1900s. **Original** stories told in comic book form started coming out in the 1930s. In 1938, *Action Comics* #1 introduced the world to Superman!

GET THE FACTS

Today, not all comics are funny, though the name has stuck.

Many people picture superheroes when they think of comic books. But many other stories have been told, including the adventures of a boy named Archie!

STAN LEE AND JACK KIRBY

In 2025, *Fantastic Four: First Steps* hit movie theaters. This idea for this team of four superheroes started more than 60 years ago in the minds of writer Stan Lee and artist Jack Kirby. Soon after, they and another artist, Steve Ditko, also created Spider-Man.

In these early days of Marvel Comics, the writers and artists worked together to figure out the story and **characters**. Lee wrote superheroes who also had feelings and problems. Kirby and Ditko created famous looks that fans still know today.

GET THE FACTS

Lee wrote several books about comics including *Origins of Marvel Comics* and *Stan Lee and the Rise and Fall of the American Comic Book*.

One comic book of *The Fantastic Four* or other superhero from Marvel Comics would tell part of a story. Readers had to wait for the next **issue** to find out what happened next. Comic book companies still put out some comics this way today!

JIM DAVIS

Jim Davis is the cartoonist behind the beloved comic strip character Garfield. As a kid, he liked to draw a lot. He studied art and business in college. Then, he worked for another comic creator. He learned how to make a comic strip and wanted to try his own ideas out.

Davis's *Garfield*, featuring a grumpy orange cat who loves lasagna, first came out in newspapers in 1978. It went on to appear in thousands of newspapers weekly!

GET THE FACTS

Before he started drawing *Garfield*, Davis looked at other popular comic strips. He noticed there wasn't anything about a pet cat. He thought this would make his work stand out.

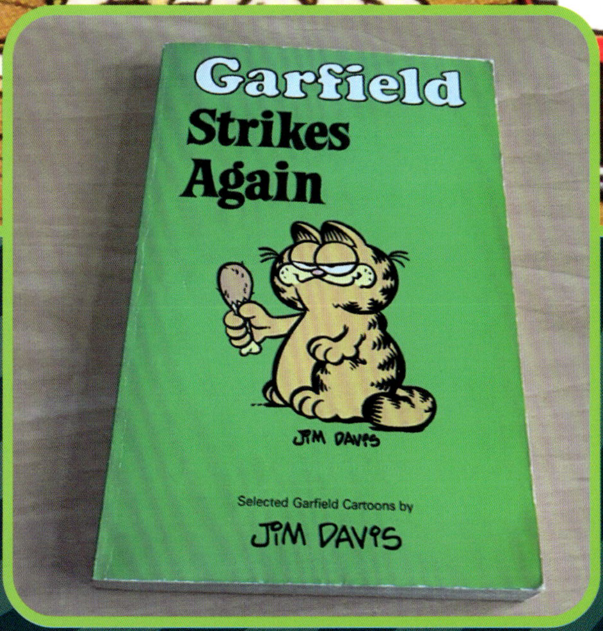

Many *Garfield* comic strips have been collected into short books.

TWO ARTS, COMBINED

Comic creation combines storytelling and writing with art. Sometimes that means a writer and artist work together—like Stan Lee and Jack Kirby. Jim Davis, on the other hand, both drew and wrote the words that went into *Garfield*.

Comic creators have to map out their story, define their characters, decide the style of their art, and choose word containers for their characters. Each step of this process takes time. Working with a friend can make it more fun—and spark more ideas!

GET THE FACTS

The words and pictures in a comic work together. Words can tell what's happening in the picture or offer more than what's shown in the picture, such as a character's thoughts.

A word container is what encloses, or holds, the text in a comic. Creators may use speech bubbles, such as those shown here.

GET INSPIRED!

Are you unsure what you want to make a comic about? Head to your school or community library and talk to the librarian. They can point you toward some collections of comic strips and graphic novels written just for kids. These may **inspire** you!

Then, keep your eyes open and look at your life! Silly things your parents do, games you make up with your friends, and odd things that happen at the park or grocery store may all be the spark that starts your comic story.

GET THE FACTS

Graphic novels often look a lot like comics and may use panels and word containers. But, unlike comics, they are the length of a book and tell a complete story.

Graphic novels, such as the *Dog Man* series, have a lot in common with comics!

MAKE A COMIC!

No comic book creator started out by writing a whole comic book in one go! They probably started with a small idea. Here are some prompts that might spark your creativity:

- Draw the funniest thing that's ever happened to you.
- Imagine a road trip with your family—and everything that could go wrong.
- Draw what you might look like as a superhero. Add a sidekick! What adventures might you go on?
- Write and draw a story from the point of view of your cat, dog, lizard, or other pet.

TRY THIS!

Using the ideas above, write a prompt for GenAI to create a comic. Draw your own **version**. What's different between the two? What do you like about yours? What do you like about the AI version?

It's OK if the first draft, or try, of your comic doesn't come out exactly right. Keep trying! It takes time and practice to get really good at creating comics.

GLOSSARY

character: Someone that appears in a comic, book, or movie.

express: To make known.

inspire: To cause someone to want to do something.

issue: A part of a story put out at one time.

original: The first of its kind.

technology: Using science, engineering, and other industries to invent useful tools or to solve problems. Also a machine, piece of equipment, or method created by technology.

unique: One of a kind.

version: A form of something that is different from others.

FOR MORE INFORMATION

BOOKS

Forney, Ellen. *Adventures of You! How to Write, Draw, and Star in Your Own Comics.* Canada: Workman Kids, 2025.

Shaskan, Stephen. *Pizza and Taco: Draw Your Own Comic!* New York, NY: Random House, 2025.

Sliney, Will. *Draw with Will.* London, UK: Gallery Kids, 2025.

WEBSITES

Learn to Make a 4-Panel Comic
imaginationsoup.net/learn-make-4-panel-comic-kids
Follow some simple steps to making your first comic.

2024 Best Graphic Novels for Children Reading List
www.ala.org/gncrt/2024-best-graphic-novels-children-reading-list#top-ten
Look for your next favorite graphic novel on this list of the American Library Association's best of 2024.

Publisher's note to educators and parents: Our editors have carefully reviewed these websites to ensure that they are suitable for students. Many websites change frequently, however, and we cannot guarantee that a site's future contents will continue to meet our high standards of quality and educational value. Be advised that students should be closely supervised whenever they access the internet.

INDEX